CW01467438

better together*

* This book is best read together, grownup and kid.

a | **akidsco.com**

a
kids
book
about

a
kids
book
about
STRESS

by Sam Wilt, LCSW-C

DK | Penguin Random House

a

A Kids Co.
Editor Jennifer Goldstein and Emma Wolf
Designer Rick DeLucco
Creative Director Rick DeLucco
Studio Manager Kenya Feldes
Sales Director Melanie Wilkins
Head of Books Jennifer Goldstein
CEO and Founder Jelani Memory

DK
Senior Production Editor Jennifer Murray
Senior Production Controller Louise Minihane
Senior Acquisitions Editor Katy Flint
Acquisitions Project Editor Sara Forster
Managing Art Editor Vicky Short
Managing Director, Licensing Mark Searle

First American edition, 2025
Published in the United States by DK Publishing, 1745 Broadway, 20th Floor,
New York, NY 10019

First published in Great Britain in 2025 by
Dorling Kindersley Limited, 20 Vauxhall Bridge Road, London SW1V 2SA
A Penguin Random House Company

The authorised representative in the EEA is
Dorling Kindersley Verlag GmbH. Arnulfstr. 124, 80636 Munich, Germany

Copyright © 2025 Dorling Kindersley Limited
A Kids Book About, Kids Are Ready, and the colophon 'a' are trademarks of A Kids Book About, Inc.
10 9 8 7 6 5 4 3 2 1
001-349871-March/2025
All rights reserved.
No part of this publication may be reproduced, stored in or introduced into a retrieval system,
or transmitted, in any form, or by any means (electronic, mechanical, photocopying, recording,
or otherwise), without the prior written permission of the copyright owner.

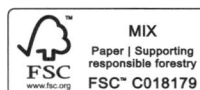

A catalog record for this book is available from the Library of Congress.
A CIP catalogue record for this book is available from the British Library.
ISBN: 978-0-2417-4329-4

DK books are available at special discounts when purchased in bulk for sales
promotions, premiums, fund-raising, or education use. For details, contact:
DK Publishing Special Markets, 1745 Broadway, 20th Floor, New York, NY 10019
SpecialSales@dk.com

Printed and bound in China
www.dk.com
akidsco.com

MIX
Paper | Supporting
responsible forestry
FSC™ C018179

This book was made with Forest
Stewardship Council™ certified
paper – one small step in DK's
commitment to a sustainable future.
Learn more at **www.dk.com/uk/
information/sustainability**

For my violinist and aspiring astronaut.
I dream of a future full of love, peace,
and happiness for you both.

Intro
for grownups

Stress is universal. In today's world, many people experience stress as a constant state of being. How do we define stress? How can we teach our children to manage their own stress and thrive when we don't do the same?

We live in a world where feeling stressed-out and overwhelmed is considered normal. Where it's more important to be productive than to truly care for yourself. In a world where exhaustion and burnout run rampant, we tend to ignore the impact it's having on our bodies, our minds, and our quality of life.

This book is about defining stress, owning it, and taking control of it. It's about starting a conversation between grownups and kids about what it is and what to do about it. My hope is that this book creates connections which lead to a future filled with more understanding and less stress.

STRESS.

Did you know everyone experiences stress?

Old people, young people, EVEN BABIES.

You've probably heard of it.

Whether you realize it or not,
you've felt it at some point.

You might call something stressful, or say that you're feeling stressed, or that you're "stressed out."

SOMETIMES,

even looking at the word can
make you feel stressed!

But what is it?

YOU MAY

YOU MAY

YOU MAY

YOU MAY

FEEL STRESS

when trying to do something challenging.

FEEL STRESS

when you have too much going on.

FEEL STRESS

just talking with someone.

FEEL STRESS

when you see the color red,
or orange, or bright yellow.

Sometimes sounds can be stressful, like a baby crying or the siren on a firetruck.

BUT WHAT IS IT?

Stress is hard to define.

So, let's talk about what stress

FEELS LIKE.

It can be kind of an icky feeling in your belly, or a tightness in your muscles.

Sometimes stress can make
you feel like it's hard to breathe.

Sometimes stress feels like
NOTHING AT ALL.

STRESS FEELS DIFFERENT FOR EACH OF US.

It even feels different for each of us at different times.

And because of this, no one can tell you whether something is stressful *for you*.

IT'S ABOUT HOW

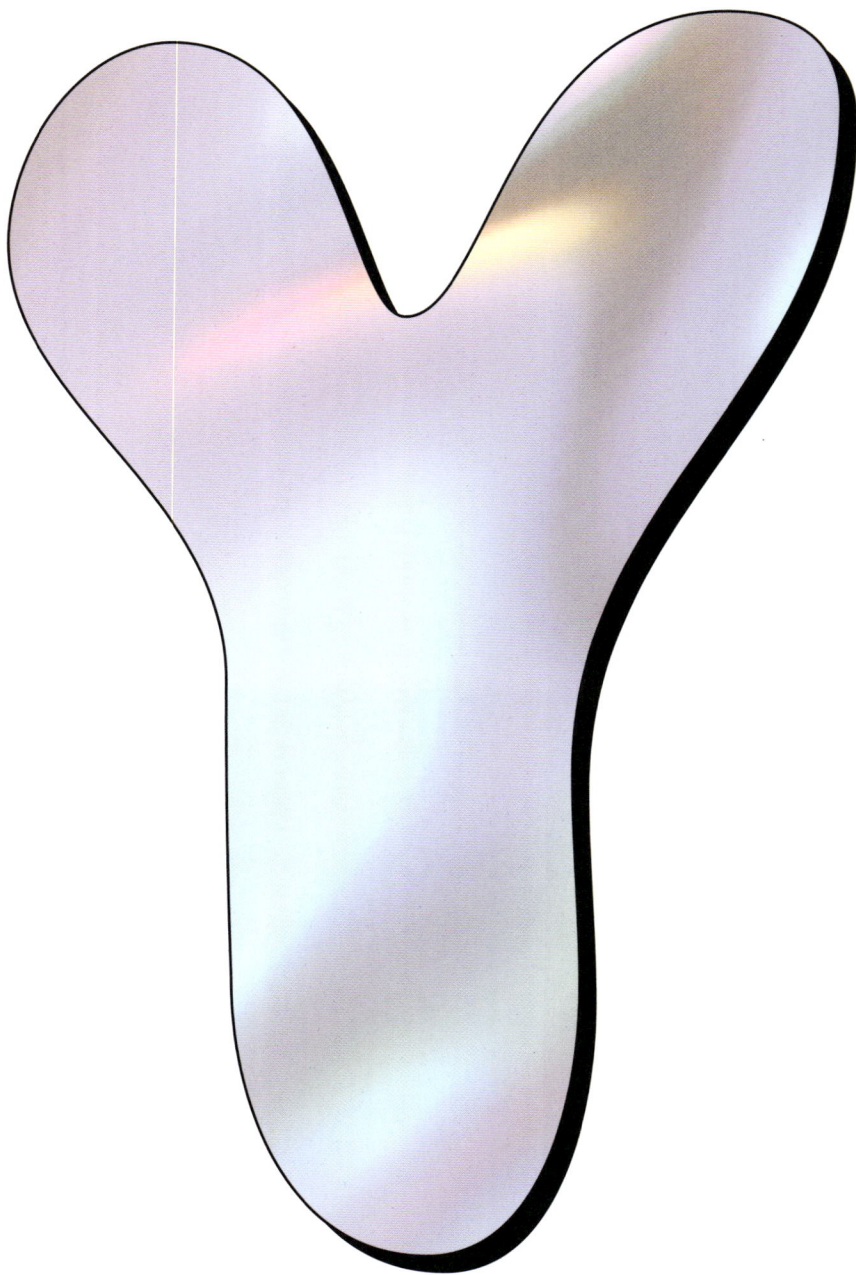
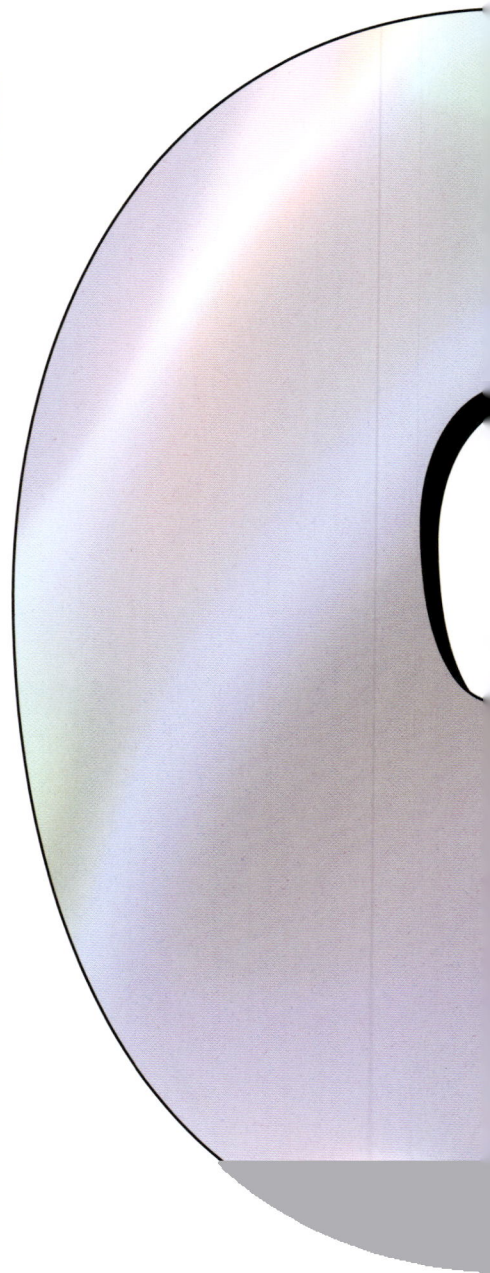

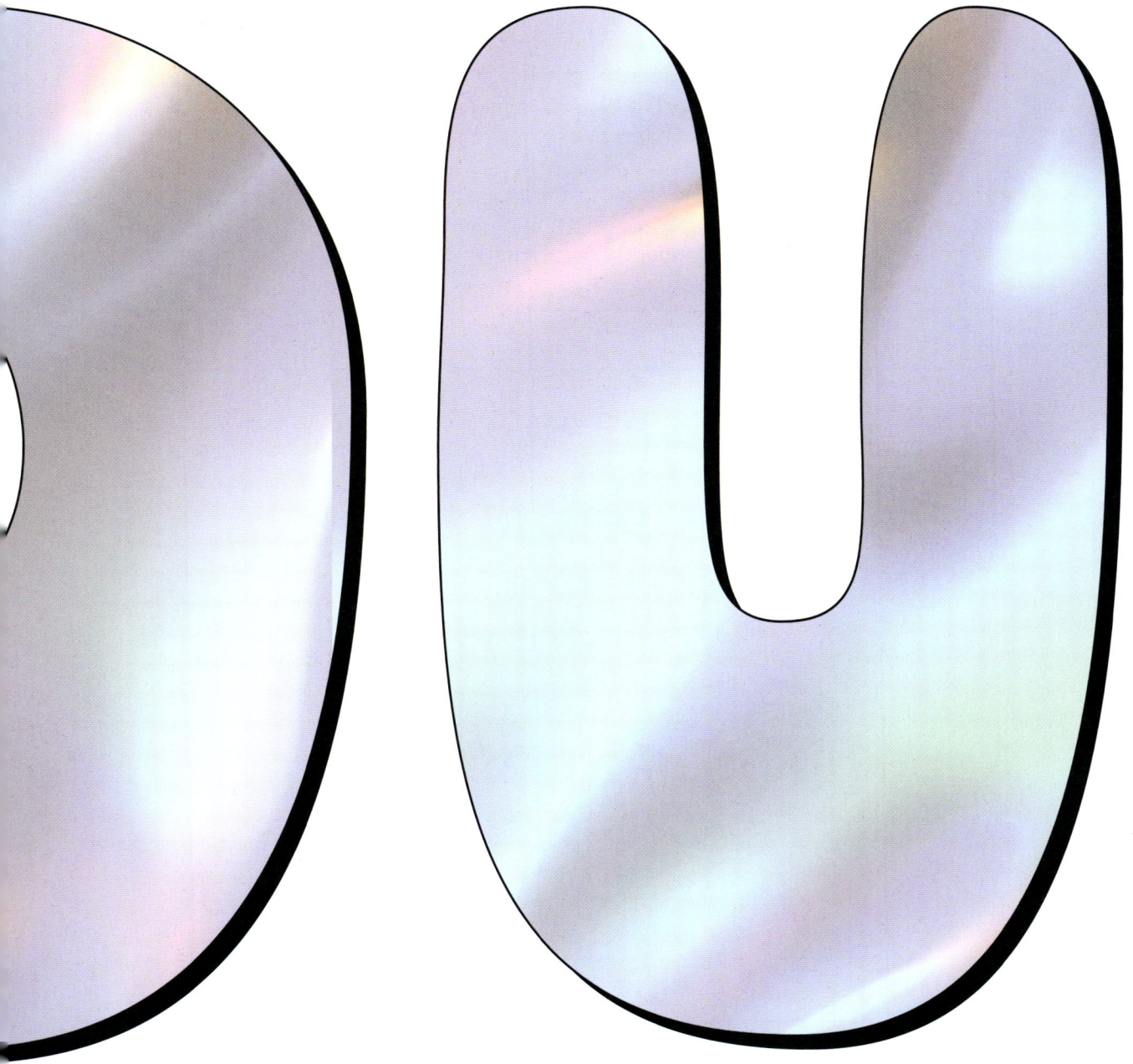

U

FEEL.

For instance, one of my favorite things to do is to read. It's fun for me!

Reading all of the time? I would LOVE that.

But some people aren't strong readers, and reading can be stressful to think about.

MAYBE you think camping sounds fun, and sleeping outside is extra special.

MAYBE you love to play the violin, especially in front of your whole class.

MAYBE you like to play soccer and get excited to score a goal.

MAYBE you are in the school play and have a really big part.

MAYBE you dream of becoming an astronaut and going into space one day.

MAYBE some of these things sound really hard and not-so-great.

MAYBE reading about all of these exciting things is starting to stress you out. (Honestly, me, too!)

Notice what's happening in your body.

Stress is your body reacting to pressure from the world around you.

Stress is a normal response that happens because your body thinks you are in danger—even when you're not.

Think about it this way:
what do you think of when
you think about feeling calm?

What does calm look like to you?

What kinds of things
help you feel calm?

Can you picture yourself somewhere
that is completely calm?

Let's call it a calm place.

When you feel stressed, you leave that calm place, and that can make it hard to notice the changes in your body.

When you feel stress,
you might feel things

MORE

OR LESS

than you do when you are calm.

You might get tense and feel worried.

You might want to be by yourself.

You might yell or cry.

You might want to sleep.

You might not be able to sleep at all.

You might feel your body shaking or your heart beating really fast.

When you notice your stress and how your body responds to it, then you can actually do something about it.

Let's talk about a few things you can do!

BREATHE.

Stress causes us to take quicker, shorter breaths.

Deep breathing gives us more oxygen, which is a good thing.

Taking deep breaths helps our bodies get the oxygen we need to think clearly and calmly.

Even just 3 deep breaths when you're feeling stressed can go a long way!

TALK TO SOMEONE.

We need other people in our lives who care about us. Human connection is super important.

These people can be family, friends, teachers, coaches, or social workers (like me).

When you talk to someone you trust about your stress, it can help you feel better.

REST.

Humans are not robots.

We cannot keep going
and going without resting
our bodies and minds.

And rest doesn't just mean sleep!

Rest can be doing something
you enjoy, or it can be something
calming like going for a walk
or taking a warm bath.

Stress can make us forget
how much we need rest.

With rest, our bodies
can disconnect from stress
and get a chance to heal.

HAVE FUN.

Being too serious for too long can make us feel stressed.

Sometimes, we forget to have fun (grownups especially!).

Did you know that laughing helps get rid of stress? Even *pretend* laughing can do that!

Try it! Yes, right now! Laugh!

Go **HA HA HA!**
Maybe **HEE HEE HEE.**
Try a little **HO HO HO.**
(Santa, is that you?)

How did that make you feel?
I bet it felt pretty good, didn't it?

Here's the thing: a lot of times, we feel stressed about things that are out of our control.

Like...

WHAT THE WEATHER
WILL BE LIKE TOMORROW,

WHETHER WE'LL FEEL SICK,

OR WHEN WE HAVE A
HARD TIME FALLING ASLEEP.

Things like these are out of your control.

If you don't have control over them,

THEN WHY STRESS OVER THEM?

This is my advice: try focusing on things you CAN control.

If the weather is bad, you can wear a coat or use an umbrella.

If you get sick you can go to the doctor.*

If you can't sleep at night, try some of your strategies for dealing with stress (deep breathing works great here!).

*If someone hurts you, tell a safe grownup.

So, what do I want you
to know about stress?

STRESS IS NORMAL. EVERYONE FEELS STRESSED SOMETIMES.

There are lots of ways to deal with stress, and there isn't a right or wrong way (as long as no one gets hurt).

You might not be able to control the things that cause you stress, but you can control how you react to them.

And here's a big one:

The best way to deal with stress is to

TAKE CARE OF

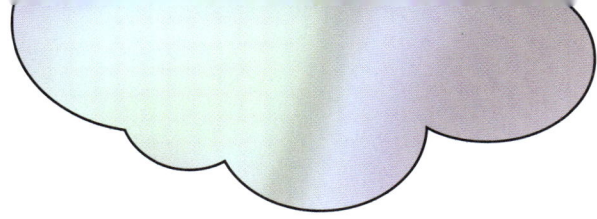

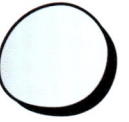

YOU.

Outro
for grownups

Keep talking. Now that you've made it through this book about stress, keep the conversation going (kids and grownups). Talk to the people in your life about stress. Talk about how it feels for you and what helps you when you feel stressed. Work together and make a list of strategies for dealing with stress. Try some of those together, and keep note of what helps and what doesn't. (There's nothing wrong with trying something and learning that it doesn't work for you!)

When grownups take the time to talk to kids about their experiences, it helps to build an understanding that they take with them into the future. Talking about how you manage stress and how you've experienced the impact of stress in your life can help kids learn how to manage their own stress.

About The Author

Sam Wilt, LCSW-C (she/her), works as a therapist, specializing in trauma and neurodivergence. Growing up, Sam always felt unseen and misunderstood. She mistook accolades as self-worth, and learned to mask who she really was to fit in. Now, she strives to live unapologetically as her true self by learning to slow down, set realistic goals, and above all else, be kind to herself.

A recovering overachiever, Sam is on a personal journey to understand and reduce the impact of stress in the world around her. She hopes to build a world that is kinder and more understanding and believes there's no such thing as a bad kid.

@ luminousgrowththerapy   in @sam-wilt-lcsw-c-cctp

🌐 luminousgrowth.com

Made to empower.

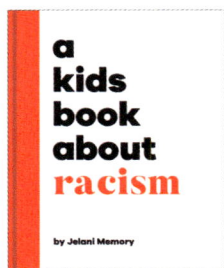

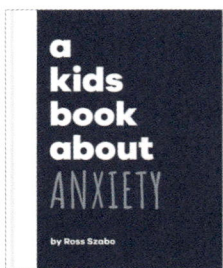

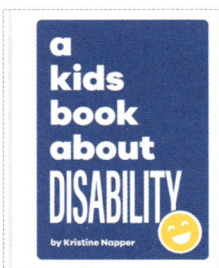

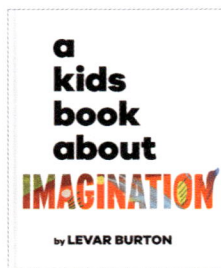

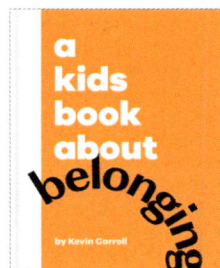

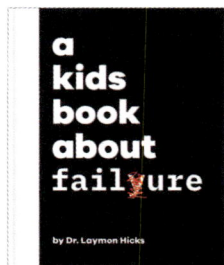

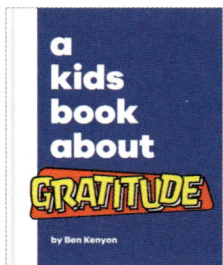

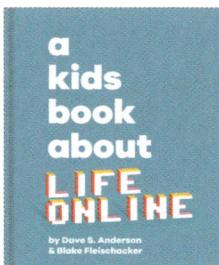

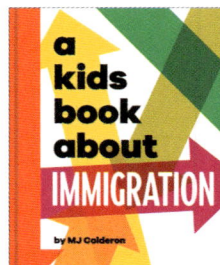

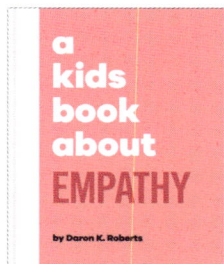

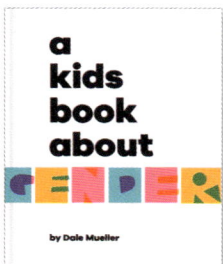

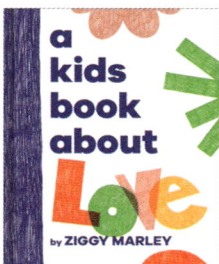

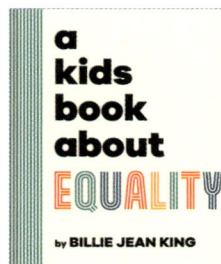

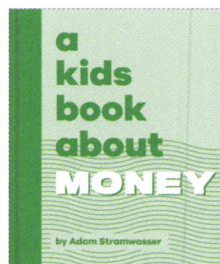

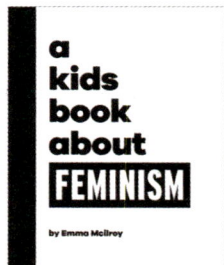

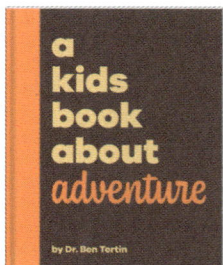

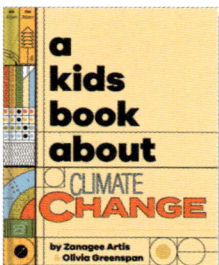

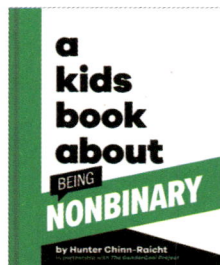

a kids book about **racism**
by Jelani Memory

a kids book about ANXIETY
by Ross Szabo

a kids book about DISABILITY
by Kristine Napper

a kids book about IMAGINATION
by LEVAR BURTON

a kids book about belonging
by Kevin Carroll

a kids book about failure
by Dr. Laymon Hicks

a kids book about GRATITUDE
by Ben Kenyon

a kids book about LIFE ONLINE
by Dave S. Anderson & Blake Fleischacker

a kids book about body image
by Rebecca Alexander

a kids book about IMMIGRATION
by MJ Calderon

a kids book about EMPATHY
by Daron K. Roberts

a kids book about GENDER
by Dale Mueller

a kids book about Love
by ZIGGY MARLEY

a kids book about EQUALITY
by BILLIE JEAN KING

a kids book about MONEY
by Adam Stramwasser

a kids book about FEMINISM
by Emma McIlroy

a kids book about adventure
by Dr. Ben Tertin

a kids book about CLIMATE CHANGE
by Zanagee Artis & Olivia Greenspan

a kids book about CONFIDENCE
by Joy Cho

a kids book about BEING NONBINARY
by Hunter Chinn-Raicht

Discover more at akidsco.com